FEEDING TO DIGESTION

Design	David West
	Children's Book Design
Designer	Flick Killerby
Editorial Planning	Clark Robinson
	Limited
Science Editor	Catherine Warren
Researcher	Emma Krikler
Illustrator	Creative Hands
Consultant	Vivienne Lee,
	physiologist

© Aladdin Books 1991

First published in
the United States in 1992 by
Gloucester Press Inc.
95 Madison Avenue
New York, NY 10016

Library of Congress Cataloging-in-Publication Data

Hemsley, William.
    Feeding to digestion : projects with biology / by William Hemsley.
        p.   cm. -- (Hands on science)
    Includes index.
    Summary: Discusses feeding methods used in the animal kingdom;
nutrition and the components of a healthy diet; and food webs of
herbivores, carnivores, parasites, and symbionts. Features projects
throughout.
    ISBN 0-531-17327-5
    1. Animals--Food--Juvenile literature. 2. Animal nutrition--Juvenile
literature. 3. Food chains (Ecology)--Juvenile literature. [1. Animals-
-Food. 2. Animal nutrition. 3. Food chains (Ecology)] I. Title. II. Series.
QL756.5.H46   1992
591.1'3--dc20   91-35075   CIP   AC

Printed in Belgium

HANDS · ON · SCIENCE

FEEDING TO DIGESTION

William Hemsley

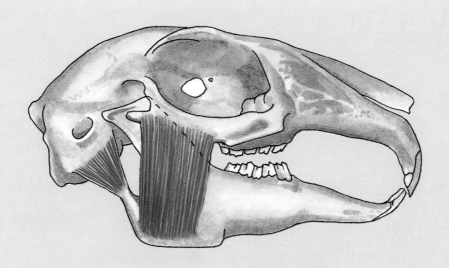

GLOUCESTER PRESS
London · New York · Toronto · Sydney

CONTENTS

This book is about the ways in which animals feed and digest their food. It tells you about the types of food that animals eat, how they find their food, and the ways in which they eat and store food. It also tells you about the feeding relationships between different animals that feed on each other. There are "hands on" projects for you to try and "did you know?" panels of information for fun.

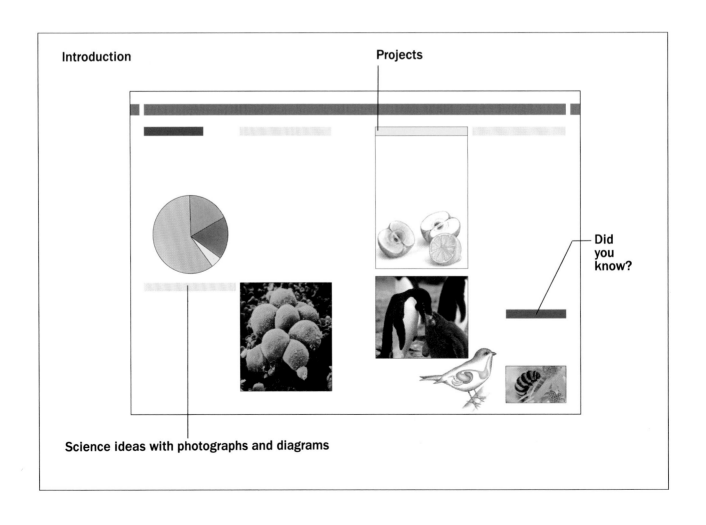

Introduction

Projects

Did you know?

Science ideas with photographs and diagrams

INTRODUCTION

Feeding is essential to the lives of all animals. Many animals spend most of their time searching for and eating food. All animals would die if they did not eat food at some stage in their lives. There is a huge variety of methods of finding food and of types of food eaten. Many of these practices are different from the ways in which humans feed.

Many of the physical characteristics of animals that you can see are connected with feeding; for example, the sharp teeth of a dog, or the beak of a bird. Other examples include strong legs to run fast and catch another animal. A large number of animals have features that are designed to prevent themselves from being eaten; for example, markings that make an animal difficult to see.

Once an animal has eaten food, it must digest it. The digestive systems of animals vary greatly. There are different problems in digesting various types of food.

A European great tit's beak can break open peanut shells.

There are two main types of food. Inorganic food consists of simple substances, such as mineral salts and carbon dioxide. Organic food consists of complex carbon-containing substances, such as proteins, carbohydrates and fats. There are also two main methods of feeding: autotrophic and heterotrophic.

AUTOTROPHIC FEEDING

Autotrophic organisms (autotrophs) are able to make organic substances from inorganic food. Inorganic food consists of simple molecules, which contain just a few atoms. Organic food consists of large, complex molecules (which are called "organic" because they are characteristic of living organisms).

Only plants and some bacteria are autotrophic. They can make organic molecules by a process known as photosynthesis (although some bacteria use rather different processes). In photosynthesis, an organism uses the energy of sunlight to make organic materials from carbon dioxide and water.

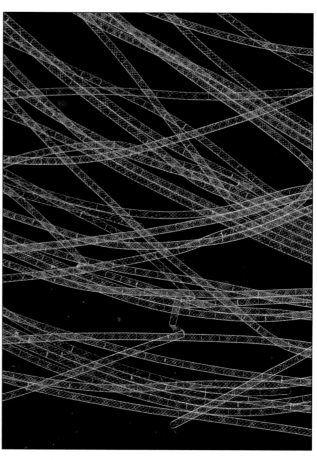

△ Spyrogyra is a tiny plant made up of strings of single cells. Like other plants, it is an autotrophic feeder.

△ Fungi look like plants, but cannot photosynthesize and so are heterotrophic feeders.

HETEROTROPHIC FEEDING

Heterotrophic organisms (heterotrophs) are not able to make organic substances from inorganic food. They have to eat organic food in order to survive. The main reason is that heterotrophs get all of their energy from organic food. They cannot get energy from sunlight by photosynthesis in the way that autotrophic organisms do. Heterotrophs also get almost all of their inorganic food by feeding on other organisms — both autotrophs and other heterotrophs.

Animals are the main group of heterotrophs. There are a few others, such as fungi. All are organisms that cannot photosynthesize. This book is about feeding in animals and so talks about heterotrophic feeding.

MAJOR NUTRIENTS

There are three types of food described as major nutrients: carbohydrates, fats and proteins. These three are all organic foods. They consist of complex molecules that contain large amounts of carbon together with a variety of other chemical substances.

Carbohydrates contain only carbon, hydrogen and oxygen. There is a wide variety of carbohydrates. The main difference between them is the length of their molecules. Small carbohydrates include sugars. The sugar used in cooking is one example; glucose is another. Large carbohydrates include starch, found in great amounts in such foods as potatoes and grains. Large carbohydrate molecules may be hundreds of times longer than small ones. Animals use carbohydrates mostly for energy.

Fats, like carbohydrates, contain only carbon, hydrogen and oxygen, but arranged very differently. Biological oils are fats that are liquid at room temperature. Animals use fats as an energy store. Fats are found in large amounts in meat, milk and many seeds. They contain more energy per gram than carbohydrates do, but cannot be used so easily.

Proteins contain carbon, hydrogen, oxygen and nitrogen. Some also contain sulfur and other substances. Proteins are made up of building blocks called amino acids. There are about 20 different amino acids. They join together to make hundreds of different proteins, most containing more than 50 amino acids. The differences between proteins depend on the order in which the amino acids are joined together. Proteins have many functions, which include the formation of muscle and other tissues, and taking part in a large number of chemical reactions.

▷ Seeds are a good source of food and contain all of the major nutrients.

▽ Meat contains large amounts of protein and fat, but little carbohydrate.

PROJECT

You can test food to see whether it contains large amounts of fat. Take a sheet of light-colored paper. Now rub a small amount of the food you have chosen on the paper (use food that is going to be thrown away). Now hold the paper up to the window or a lamp. If the food consists mostly of fat, the paper will let more light through where you rubbed it.

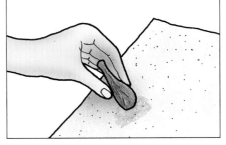

MINERALS

Minerals are inorganic food. They are described as minor nutrients, together with vitamins. The minerals that an animal needs are commonly found in nonliving material. But animals usually get all of their minerals by eating living things that contain the minerals. Animals use only small amounts of minerals, but a shortage leads to deficiency diseases.

Some of the minerals needed by mammals (such as humans) are as follows. Only some of the main functions are described.
- Calcium: used in bones and teeth
- Phosphorus: used in bones and teeth, and in producing energy from food
- Iron: part of hemoglobin, which carries oxygen and carbon dioxide in the blood
- Potassium: needed for nerves to work
- Sodium: needed for nerves to work
- Iodine: part of the body substance that controls growth
- Fluorine: needed to make teeth and bones, and to prevent tooth decay

Other minerals needed include sulfur, chlorine, magnesium, zinc, copper, manganese, chromium and cobalt.

VITAMINS

Vitamins are organic foods. Animals need them in very small amounts, but vitamins are extremely important. They are mostly involved in helping and controlling chemical reactions in the body. As with minerals, a lack of vitamins in the diet leads to deficiency diseases; for instance, a lack of vitamin C causes scurvy. Not all animals need the same vitamins; for example, humans need vitamin C, but most animals can make their own. Vitamins come from a wide variety of foods, although some foods have more of some vitamins than of others.

The vitamins are as follows. Only some of their main functions are given.
- Vitamin A: healthy skin and eyes, and resistance to disease
- Vitamin B: there are at least ten B vitamins, which are involved in many functions, but especially in the production of energy from food
- Vitamin C: repair to damaged tissues
- Vitamin D: healthy bones
- Vitamin E: affects reproduction in some animals (but not in humans)
- Vitamin K: helps with blood clotting

DID YOU KNOW?

The human body contains as much calcium as 340 sticks of chalk, as much phosphorus and sulfur as 2,500 boxes of matches, potassium as 4.5 pounds of fertilizer, sodium and chlorine as 40 teaspoonsful of salt, magnesium as in 80 indigestion tablets, iron as 6 paper clips, fluoride as 30 tubes of toothpaste, and zinc as a small battery. The rest of the minerals in the body would fill about one-tenth of a teaspoon.

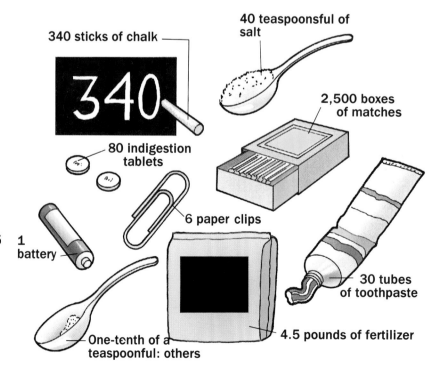

340 sticks of chalk

40 teaspoonsful of salt

2,500 boxes of matches

80 indigestion tablets

6 paper clips

1 battery

30 tubes of toothpaste

One-tenth of a teaspoonful: others

4.5 pounds of fertilizer

△ Many animals must drink water to survive.

▽ Elephants get large amounts of fiber when eating wood.

WATER

A very large part of the body of every animal is water. Water has many functions. All chemical reactions in the body take place in water. Substances are carried around the body by watery fluids. Water is involved in temperature control (for example, when an animal sweats), and is important for many other reasons.

Animals obtain water in three ways. First, they can drink it directly — for example, from a pool or stream. Second, they can obtain it from the food they eat. Some animals get all of their water in this way and never drink at all. Third, animals that live in a watery environment can simply absorb water through their skins.

OTHER SUBSTANCES

In addition to the major nutrients, minor nutrients and water, there are other substances that animals take in.

Dietary fiber (also known as roughage) consists of the indigestible or poorly digestible parts of food. It is made up mostly of the cell walls of plants. Fiber gives solidity to food and increases the overall rate at which food passes through the intestine.

Different animals require different amounts of fiber. Animals that eat mostly meat get very little fiber, but need only a little. Animals that eat plants get much more, although they can usually digest plant cell walls to some degree. In animals that need fiber, a sufficient amount in the diet helps to prevent some disorders of the intestines.

Many birds — especially those that eat seeds — swallow small stones. They take the stones into their gizzards to help them grind up food. Hens eat egg shells. They are able to reabsorb the minerals to make shells for new eggs. Some animals lick salt from the ground, where it is sometimes found as a natural mineral.

Animals may eat substances that are of no use to the body. Food may contain indigestible parts, such as bone. It may contain chemicals that have no nutritional value. Food that has been accidentally eaten may even contain poisons.

Animals are heterotrophic feeders — they must feed on other organisms (see page 6). Some animals eat plants (and are known as herbivores); some eat animals (carnivores); and some eat both (omnivores). The relationships between animals, the food they eat, and the animals that eat them are very complex.

FOOD CHAINS

The simplest way to look at food relationships is by a food chain. The best way to understand food chains is to use an example.

A field has grass growing in it. Crickets live in the field and eat the grass. The crickets are eaten by lizards, which are in turn eaten by hawks.

This example of a food chain has four "links" in it. The first link, the grass, produces the nutrients needed in the chain. These nutrients include both energy and such things as minerals. The grass produces the nutrients by using energy from the sun and by absorbing minerals from the soil. The grass is therefore known as a producer.

The other links in the chain are known as consumers. They get the energy and nutrients they need from an organism lower down the chain. The first consumer in the chain must be a herbivore. Higher links are carnivores. An omnivore might be any link in the chain.

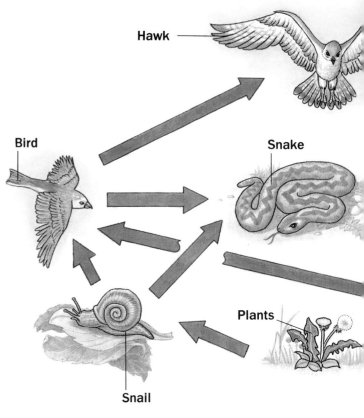

Hawk
Snake
Bird
Plants
Snail

PYRAMIDS

Another way to look at food chains is as a pyramid of numbers or of biomass. Three examples of pyramids are illustrated below. A pyramid of numbers shows the number of each organism. A pyramid of biomass shows the total mass (or weight) of the organisms. At the bottom of a pyramid is a producer. Each stage up the pyramid is a link in the food chain.

The pyramid becomes smaller toward the top because at each stage the chain

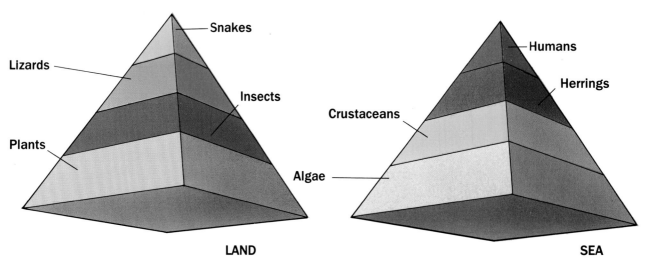

Snakes
Lizards
Insects
Plants

LAND

Humans
Herrings
Crustaceans
Algae

SEA

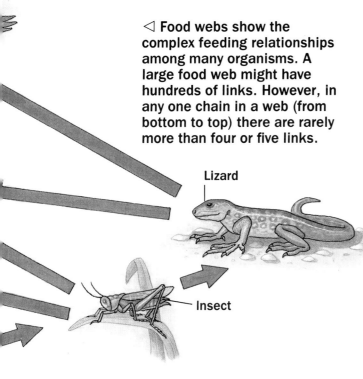

◁ Food webs show the complex feeding relationships among many organisms. A large food web might have hundreds of links. However, in any one chain in a web (from bottom to top) there are rarely more than four or five links.

Lizard

Insect

WEBS AND CYCLES

Food chains give a quite simple picture of feeding relationships. But in reality, the relationships are usually much more complex. Most animals feed on more than one other organism, and are eaten by more than one type of animal. Food webs try to show all of the relationships, or at least a large part of them. A food web is like a large number of food chains, all combined together.

The parts of a web are closely linked, and a change in one part can affect many others. If the numbers of one organism get fewer, so will the numbers of the organisms that feed on it. On the other hand, those organisms it eats may increase in numbers. For example, the Canadian lynx relies on the snowshoe hare for a large part of its diet. When the population of the hare drops, the population of the lynx drops soon afterward. When the population of the hare rises, so does that of the lynx.

Most of the nutrients in a food web are recycled. For example, when an animal dies, it decomposes; the chemicals it contains return to the soil and can be reabsorbed by plants. But energy is lost — for example, as heat from an animal's body. Energy must be replaced by producers, taking energy from the sun.

loses nutrients. A large amount of the food that an animal eats is used up. In particular, food that contains energy is used up when an animal uses energy (for example, by moving). Other food is lost when an animal eats more than it needs.

Pyramids of biomass are more useful than pyramids of numbers. For example, a hundred fleas may feed on a dog. But the total weight of fleas would be much less than the weight of the dog, and they would use up far fewer nutrients.

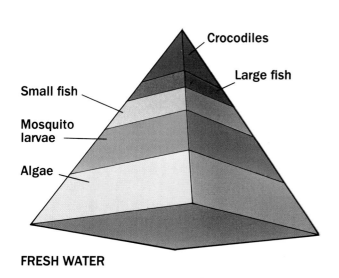

Crocodiles

Large fish

Small fish

Mosquito larvae

Algae

FRESH WATER

△ The Canadian lynx feeds on the snowshoe hare.

Even the smallest animal has to feed in order to get energy and nutrients. Tiny animals can feed on nothing larger than minute particles of food floating in water. But many very large animals also feed on small food particles. Some other animals do not feed on solid food at all, but only drink liquids.

MICROORGANISMS

Microorganisms are tiny, often single-celled plants and animals. They live in water or other damp environments.

Microorganisms such as paramecia are covered in cilia, which are like tiny bundles of muscular fibers on the surface of the cell. Paramecia wave their cilia to move. This action also creates currents that draw food particles into the oral groove. A particle is then taken into the cell as a food vacuole.

Amoebas surround food particles with fingerlike extensions from the cell called pseudopodia. As in paramecia, a food particle is drawn into the cell to form a food vacuole. This can happen anywhere on the surface of an amoeba.

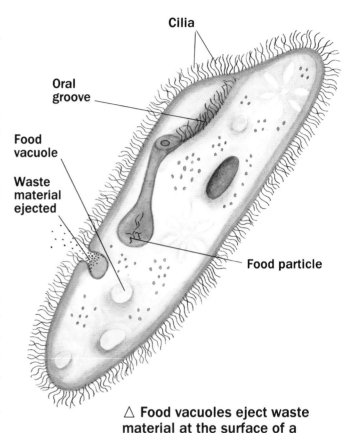

△ Food vacuoles eject waste material at the surface of a paramecium after digestion.

△ A flamingo's large beak is shaped to be held upside down in the water as it feeds.

FILTER FEEDERS

A variety of animals use filter feeding. These animals filter small particles of food from water.

Many shellfish are filter feeders. They use cilia on their gills. (Gills are normally used to get oxygen from water.) An example of such a shellfish is the mussel. Mussels draw water past their gills by moving their cilia. The gills and cilia are covered with a sticky mucus (a substance produced by the surface of the gills). The mucus traps food particles from the water. The cilia move the mucus and food particles to the mussel's mouth.

Flamingoes are unusual filter-feeding birds. They wade in shallow lakes on their long legs, while holding their beaks upside down in the water. The opening of a flamingo's beak is surrounded by bristles. The bird moves its beak from side to side, and the bristles filter minute plants and animals from the water.

Many fish, such as herrings, use filter feeding. They have structures on their gills called gill rakers. The rakers sieve food from the water that passes over the gills. The food is usually such things as small shrimp-like animals, called plankton, and the larvae of sea animals.

Some whales filter feed — for example, blue whales. They use a large number of thin plates hanging from their upper jaws to filter tiny animals from the water.

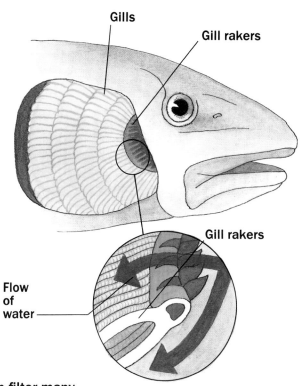

Gills

Gill rakers

Gill rakers

Flow of water

△ Gill rakers can filter many food particles from water.

DID YOU KNOW?

There is a type of spider that is colored yellow (below). The color allows it to hide in yellow flowers without being seen by bees. When a bee arrives to feed on nectar, the spider kills the bee and sucks fluid from its body.

△ Butterflies have a long proboscis, which uncurls to suck nectar from flowers.

FLUID FEEDERS

Animals that feed only on liquids are called fluid feeders. Most fluid feeders are insects. Such insects have specially designed mouthparts.

Many insects that feed on fluids are parasites — they suck blood or sap from living animals or plants (see page 22).

A number of insects feed on nectar, a sugary fluid which is made in flowers. Examples include butterflies and bees. The mouthparts of such insects usually have a long tube (called a proboscis). This tube is used to reach into flowers and suck the nectar.

Flies feed on fluid by pumping saliva onto solid food. The saliva partly digests the food and makes it liquid. The mouth then sucks up the liquid food.

A few other types of animal feed on fluids. Examples include spiders, which inject insects with digestive fluid and suck the juices out and hummingbirds, which feed on flower nectar.

Herbivores feed on plants. Different herbivores eat many different parts of plants. The main problem that herbivores have with feeding is that some plant material is difficult to digest. This is particularly a problem for mammals, because they cannot make substances that can digest cellulose.

EATING CELLULOSE

The main carbohydrate (page 7) in many parts of plants is cellulose — for example, in leaves and stems. Cellulose makes up the cell walls of plants. Herbivorous mammals have various special methods of digesting cellulose.

Most herbivorous mammals have large numbers of bacteria in their intestines which can digest cellulose. The bacteria absorb some of the digested material. But much of the material is left over for the animal to absorb.

A rabbit, for example, has such bacteria in its cecum, appendix and colon. Rabbits also help digestion by passing food through their intestines twice. They do this by eating their own feces. Rabbits extract further nutrition as the food passes through for the second time. This is called refection.

RABBIT SKULL

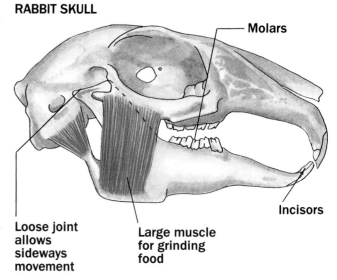

Molars

Incisors

Loose joint allows sideways movement

Large muscle for grinding food

△ Rabbits eat their own feces to get extra nutrition from plant food that is hard to digest.

▷ After food has passed through a rabbit's intestine, the feces come out as green pellets, called cetrophs. Rabbits swallow these pellets, which are digested more in the stomach than in the cecum and appendix. The feces re-emerge brown.

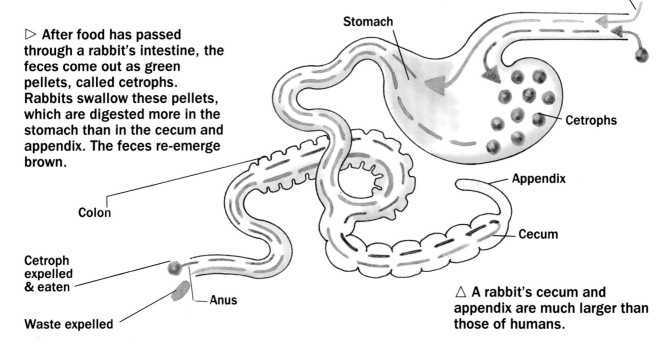

Food eaten

Stomach

Cetrophs

Appendix

Colon

Cecum

Cetroph expelled & eaten

Anus

Waste expelled

△ A rabbit's cecum and appendix are much larger than those of humans.

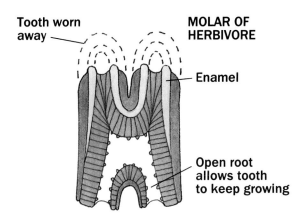

Tooth worn away

MOLAR OF HERBIVORE

Enamel

Open root allows tooth to keep growing

◁△ A rabbit's jaws and teeth are designed for breaking up tough plant food. The teeth wear down to leave hard ridges of enamel.

△ Cattle are ruminants. Their diet is largely grass.

RUMINATION AND TEETH

Many herbivores are ruminants — including sheep, cattle, deer, antelopes, goats and kangaroos. Ruminants have several pouches in their digestive passages. Food goes first to the rumen, which contains great numbers of bacteria that can digest cellulose. After some time in the rumen, the food returns to the mouth. Here the food is chewed further (this is known as rumination, or chewing the cud). The food is swallowed again and passes through the reticulum and omasum, where more digestion by bacteria takes place. When the food reaches the abomasum, any bacteria in the food are killed by acid and digested.

The teeth and jaws of herbivorous mammals are designed for breaking up plant material. The front teeth (incisors) are shaped for tearing off food. The molar teeth are designed for grinding up food. The teeth grow for all of the animal's life (unlike the teeth of carnivores). At the same time as they grow, the teeth wear down. The tops of molar teeth wear away leaving hard, sharp ridges of enamel. These ridges are very effective for grinding up tough plant food. The jaw is designed to move easily from side to side as the teeth grind the food.

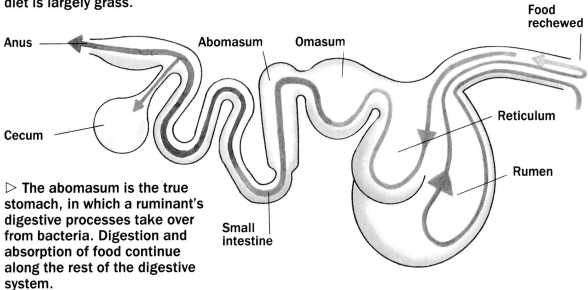

Food rechewed

Anus

Abomasum

Omasum

Reticulum

Cecum

Rumen

▷ The abomasum is the true stomach, in which a ruminant's digestive processes take over from bacteria. Digestion and absorption of food continue along the rest of the digestive system.

Small intestine

Carnivores feed on animals. There are a number of characteristics that make them different from herbivores. Many of these characteristics are of the teeth, jaws and other mouthparts. The digestive systems of carnivores are shorter than those of herbivores because meat is easier to digest than plant material.

MAMMAL CARNIVORES

The teeth of carnivores are designed for both catching and eating their prey. Dogs have teeth that are typical of carnivorous mammals. The front teeth (the incisors) are designed for gripping and tearing off pieces of meat. The canine teeth are pointed and long. They pierce the flesh of the dog's prey, stopping the prey from escaping and helping to kill it. The rest of the teeth are designed mainly for breaking up food. The large carnassial teeth move past each other like scissors, cutting through meat. The rear molars crush food into small pieces.

There is a large and powerful muscle for closing the jaws. This helps the teeth both to hold onto prey and to chew meat. The hinge of the jaw only lets the jaw move up and down, not from side to side as with herbivores. Food is therefore cut or crushed, not ground up.

△ The fox is a carnivore that feeds on a variety of small animals.

Enamel not worn down

Tooth held firmly in bone

Nearly closed root

◁△ A dog's teeth are designed for gripping prey and breaking up meat. They do not grow once they have reached full size and have a root that is almost closed. The teeth do not wear down in the way that a herbivore's teeth do.

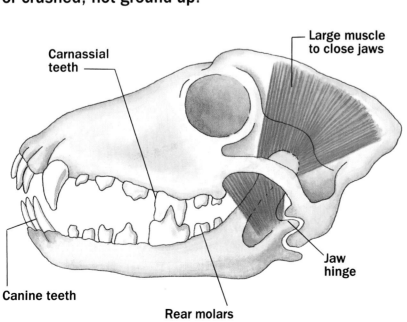

Carnassial teeth

Large muscle to close jaws

Jaw hinge

Canine teeth

Rear molars

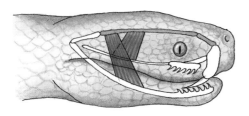

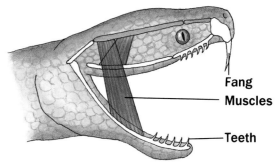

Fang
Muscles
Teeth

△ Many snakes have jaws that can open very widely. Many also have fangs that swing forward when the jaws open.

OTHER CARNIVORES

There are many types of carnivore in the animal kingdom. These animals have a variety of adaptations for eating meat.

Many carnivorous fish do not have teeth that can cut or crush food. They just have a large number of spike-like teeth for holding onto prey. Such fish swallow their prey whole. Other fish, like piranhas and many sharks, do have teeth that can tear through flesh.

Sharks are unusual because they have several rows of teeth. They use only the front two or so rows. The teeth in the other rows grow and move forward to replace the front rows of teeth.

Snakes do not have cutting teeth or strong jaws. As a result, they have to swallow their prey whole. To do this, snakes have long jawbones with loose hinges, which allow their mouths to open very widely. Many snakes can swallow prey that is bigger than their own heads.

Birds that have to tear up their prey before swallowing it have strong, hooked beaks. Such birds include vultures and birds of prey.

INSECTIVORES

Insectivores are carnivores that eat insects. Most frogs and toads have long, sticky tongues that they shoot out to catch insects. Chameleons have similar tongues, which they control with large muscles in their throats. A number of mammals, like anteaters, also have sticky tongues, which they use to pick up ants and termites. Bats and other small mammals use their teeth to catch insects. Many birds pick up insects with their beaks. Some insects are insectivores and have powerful mouthparts.

△ A three-horned chameleon.

△ Sharks have rows of teeth that move forward, replacing lost or damaged teeth.

DID YOU KNOW?

A few plants eat insects. One example is Venus's-flytrap. When an insect lands on its special leaves, the leaves snap together to trap the insect. The plant then digests its victim.

The competition between predators and prey is in some ways like a battle between armies, each with its methods of attack and defense. Predators are animals that hunt other animals (prey). Predators have many methods of catching their prey. Hunted animals have many ways of protecting themselves.

DEFENSE

Animals have a huge variety of ways of defending themselves from predators. One obvious method is by running, flying or swimming from danger. Examples of animals whose main defense is running are antelopes and zebras. Some animals also try to confuse predators while escaping. For example, rabbits make sideways jumps while they are running away.

Hiding from predators is a method of defense. Some animals live in holes in the ground. Others spend much of their time hidden among bushes or other plants. Small animals often come out of hiding only at night when it is dark.

Another way of hiding is to use camouflage. An animal's coat, fur or feathers are camouflaged by color or patterns, which often mimic their natural surroundings. For example, a brown,

△ The horned frog looks very like a dead leaf.

▷ Skunks defend themselves by spraying foul-smelling liquid from glands near their tails.

speckled pattern blends in well with twigs and dry plants in a forest. Some animals do not look like animals at all. For example, stick insects look more like twigs than like insects.

Some animals look like other, dangerous animals. For example, many hover flies have yellow and black stripes like a wasp. Predators think that they will be stung if they attack. Small animals — including some butterflies — often have large spots that resemble eyes. This may fool a predator into thinking that it is attacking a much larger animal.

Many animals fight back against predators. Large animals may kick, bite, or use horns or tusks. Some smaller animals have poisonous bites or stings. Others have foul odors or poisonous skins. Poisonous animals are often brightly colored to warn predators away.

Another form of defense is to have armor plating. Animals with such protection include shellfish, snails, turtles and armadillos. Porcupines are covered in sharp quills.

△ Spots that resemble large eyes may frighten a predator.

DETECTING PREY

Before attacking, a predator has to find its prey, which it does by using senses like smell, sight and hearing.

Sight allows predators to pinpoint their prey and observe their target's movements. Animals that attack their prey from long distances have very good eyesight. For example, hawks swoop down on their prey from the air and can see small animals, like field mice, from great heights. Animals that hunt in poor light often have large eyes to let in as much light as possible.

Hearing can be used to detect any noise that the prey makes. For most animals, hearing gives a rough idea of the direction of the prey. Bats hunt at night so cannot see prey easily. They use a system called echolocation. They let out squeaks and hear the echo from the prey. Dolphins use a similar system.

Animals also use smell to find prey. They sniff out the prey's scent in the air or on the ground. Some animals, such as dogs, can follow prey for long distances by using scent on the ground.

A large number of fish can sense the tiny electrical charges created by animals. These fish use an organ called the lateral line that runs down the sides of their bodies.

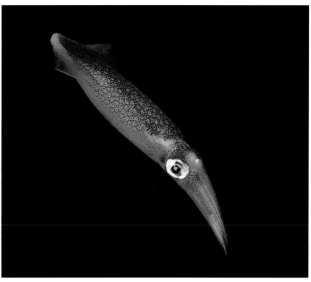

△ Cuttlefish have large eyes to see prey in dark waters.

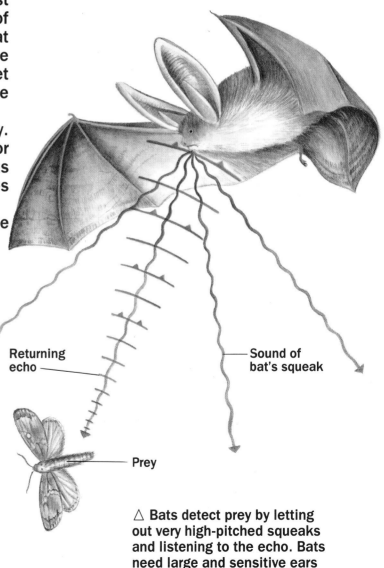

Returning echo

Sound of bat's squeak

Prey

△ Bats detect prey by letting out very high-pitched squeaks and listening to the echo. Bats need large and sensitive ears to hear the tiny sound of an echo bounce off an insect.

EXPERIMENT

Find your way by using echolocation like a bat. Stand outdoors near to a large wall. Get a friend to blindfold you and turn you around a few times. Make a sharp sound, such as banging two pieces of wood together. Can you tell in which direction the wall is by listening for the echo?

CATCHING PREY

The most common way of catching prey is to chase it. Predators often stalk their prey, trying to get as close as possible before chasing. Some predators, such as wolves, can chase their prey for quite long distances. Others, such as cheetahs, move very quickly, but can run for only short distances.

Another common method of hunting is to wait in ambush for prey. For example, leopards sometimes wait in trees and jump out onto passing animals. Birds of prey swoop down from the air before their victim has time to run away.

Most spiders use webs to catch their prey. An insect flies into the web without seeing it and becomes trapped. Ant lions also set traps. An ant lion makes a conical hole in the ground and waits at the bottom.

Many predators catch hold of their prey and kill it with their teeth, beaks, other mouthparts or claws. But there are different methods. Constrictor snakes wrap their bodies around prey and crush it to death. Other snakes use poisonous bites. Spiders, octopuses, some jellyfish and a few fish also use poison. Electric eels and some other fish use electric shocks to stun or kill their prey.

△ African wild dogs hunt in packs for buffalo.

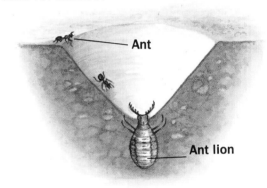

△ Ant lions wait at the bottom of their traps with only their heads showing.

△ Poisonous snakes use their fangs to inject poison.

▽ The snapping turtle lures prey into its mouth with what looks like a small worm.

USING TOOLS

Very few animals use tools to catch or kill their prey. Humans use by far the most complex and varied tools. These tools include spears, bows and guns, among many others. Chimpanzees use thin sticks to catch termites. They lick a stick and push it into a termites' nest. Then they pull the stick out covered in termites. A few types of bird, such as Darwin's finch, use thorns to pull insects out of tree bark. Sea otters break open clams and other shellfish by smashing the shells against stones. Some birds drop snails onto the ground to break the shells. Siberian crows get water to drink in the winter by dropping stones onto frozen lakes.

PACK HUNTING

There are two main advantages to hunting in packs. First, it makes hunting more efficient. Animals that are hunted can often run very quickly and are difficult for a single predator to catch. Second, pack hunting helps animals to kill prey that is much larger than themselves. For example, a pack of African wild dogs can kill a buffalo many times the size and strength of a single dog.

Only animals that live in groups hunt in packs. Examples include wolves, jackals and lions. There are many methods used for pack hunting. One method that lions use is as follows. Some of a group of lions lie hidden on one side of a herd of, for example, zebras. Other lions start to stalk the herd from the opposite side. These lions deliberately let themselves be seen. The herd moves away from what it thinks is the danger. But the hidden lions are waiting and leap out when the herd is close.

Most animals that hunt in groups are mammals. An example of another type of animal, however, is African army ants. These ants move in huge numbers and swarm over any victim that gets in their way. The ants can move only slowly and so are little danger to large animals, which can easily run away. Their prey is mainly insects and other small animals.

▽ Sea otters open clams by knocking their shells against rocks until they break.

SPIDERS' WEBS

Find a web with a spider waiting on it. Gently touch the web with a piece of grass or a thin twig. The spider will run out to catch what it thinks is an insect.

Parasites feed off living plants and animals. A parasite's victim is called the host. Most parasites cause some harm to their host, even if the harm is not serious. A number of parasites eventually kill their hosts. Some types of animal live together and help each other. This relationship is known as symbiosis.

BLOODSUCKERS

A number of insects, ticks and mites feed by sucking blood from larger animals. The insects include fleas, lice, bedbugs and mosquitoes. They all have special mouthparts for piercing skin and sucking blood. For example, the mouthparts of a female mosquito (males feed on plants) make up a long, thin tube. The labium supports the tube while the mandibles and maxillae pierce the victim's skin. The saliva duct then injects a special saliva that prevents blood from clotting (becoming solid). The mosquito sucks up blood through the labrum.

The action of sucking blood itself usually causes little harm to the host. But the saliva of bloodsucking insects can carry diseases that infect their hosts.

Leeches, a type of worm, also feed by sucking blood. They live mostly in water. Leeches attach themselves to their hosts with suckers around the mouth.

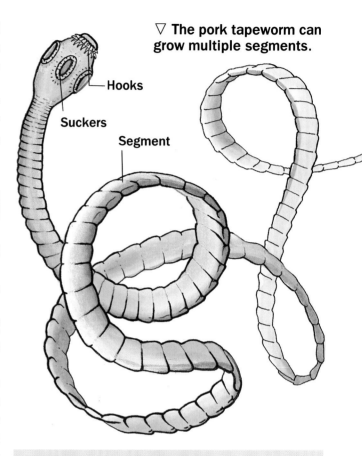

▽ The pork tapeworm can grow multiple segments.

Hooks

Suckers

Segment

INTERNAL PARASITES

Some parasites live inside their hosts. Many of these parasites are worms. For example, the pork tapeworm lives in human intestines. It absorbs digested food through its skin. The head of the worm has hooks and suckers to hold on to the intestine. Some tapeworms can grow to lengths of over 33 feet. The pork tapeworm has a complex life cycle — as do many parasitic worms. Its larvae live in the flesh of pigs. Humans may be infected if they eat undercooked pork. There are many other types of tapeworm.

Flukes are another group of parasitic worms. They can infect many parts of a host's body, including the liver, lungs and intestines. Hookworms live in the intestines of animals. They are much smaller than tapeworms and suck blood from the walls of their hosts' intestines.

Some single-celled animals are parasites and cause disease. For example, plasmodia cause malaria, and some amoebas cause amoebic dysentery.

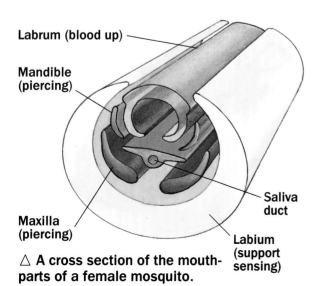

Labrum (blood up)

Mandible (piercing)

Maxilla (piercing)

Saliva duct

Labium (support sensing)

△ A cross section of the mouthparts of a female mosquito.

DID YOU KNOW?

Vampire bats drink the blood of birds and mammals. They have sharp teeth with which they cut the flesh of the animal before lapping up the blood. The bite causes little injury, but can spread disease. Vampire bats live in South America.

SYMBIOSIS

Many animals share symbiotic relation-ships. A good example among fish is the cleaner wrasse. This small fish eats parasites and dead scales on large fish, such as the sweetlips. The sweetlips is a dangerous predator, but it even allows the wrasse to swim into its mouth. The large fish benefits by being cleaned, and the wrasse benefits by having a good supply of food. Cleaner wrasses wait in particular areas so that large fish know where to go to be cleaned.

A similar example, but on land, is the crocodile bird. This bird feeds on the backs of crocodiles, keeping the croc-odile clean and free from parasites.

SAPSUCKERS

Some insects feed by sucking the sap (juices) from plants. These animals have mouthparts very similar to those of blood-sucking insects. Sapsucking insects include aphids (greenflies), plant hop-pers, froghoppers, leaf suckers, and plant lice.

Many sapsucking insects can cause much damage to crops and so are serious pests. When such insects have been accidentally brought to new countries, some crops have been almost destroyed.

△ The mouth of a sweetlips.

There is symbiosis between aphids and ants. Aphids produce a sweet liquid called honeydew. Ants feed on this fluid. In return, the ants look after and protect the aphids.

Intestines of herbivores (see page 14) and the bacteria within also have a symbiotic exchange. The animal gains by being able to digest cellulose; the bacteria have a constant supply of food.

Sometimes symbiosis seems to benefit only one of the animals. For example, a fish called the remora holds on to sharks. The remora is carried around and pro-tected. When the shark catches prey, the remora lets go and feeds on scraps of the shark's food in the water.

△ Ants protect aphids in return for honeydew.

Digestion is breaking down food so that it can be absorbed and used. Breaking down food involves mostly chemical actions on the nutrients. The human digestive system is used here as an example. It is quite typical of mammals, but is in many ways different from more distantly related animals.

THE DIGESTIVE SYSTEM

Digestion starts in the mouth. Here food is broken up by chewing and mixed with saliva. The saliva makes food easier to swallow and contains an enzyme.

Enzymes are catalysts. A catalyst is a substance that makes a chemical reaction happen more quickly, but is not itself changed in the reaction. Digestive enzymes help the chemical breakdown of food. They make the chemical reactions happen hundreds or even thousands of times faster. It is mostly major nutrients (see page 6) that must be broken down into simpler chemicals. Minor nutrients (page 8) can usually be absorbed by the intestine without changing. All animals use enzymes to digest food.

The enzyme in saliva starts to digest cooked starch. It turns the starch into a sugar, which can easily dissolve. The food is then swallowed. Muscles in the esophagus move the food down to the stomach. Muscles move food all the way through the digestive system.

Mouth

Esophagus

Liver

Stomach

Pancreas

Small intestine

Colon

Cecum and appendix

Anus

△ The organs of the human digestive system.

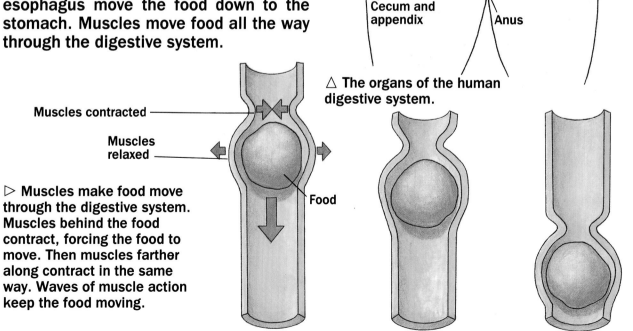

Muscles contracted

Muscles relaxed

Food

▷ Muscles make food move through the digestive system. Muscles behind the food contract, forcing the food to move. Then muscles farther along contract in the same way. Waves of muscle action keep the food moving.

▽ The stomach is made up of layers of muscles. The lining produces acid and enzymes.

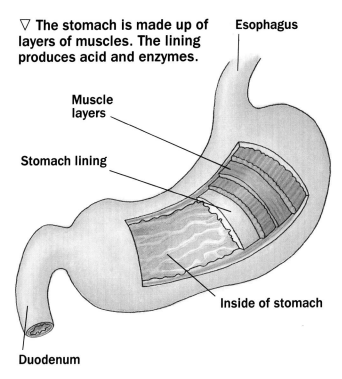

Esophagus

Muscle layers

Stomach lining

Inside of stomach

Duodenum

EXPERIMENT

Bile from the liver lets oils and fats mix with water more easily. Detergents have much the same effect. Fill a glass about half full of water. Add about three teaspoonsful of cooking oil (use some that is going to be thrown away). Mix the water and oil with a spoon. After a while, the oil will float to the surface. Now add a drop or two of dishwashing liquid. Mix again, and the water and oil will stay mixed.

Oil floats

Oil mixes with water

The stomach holds food for between one and four hours. The stomach lining produces enzymes that digest proteins, and acid that helps the enzymes to work. Muscles around the stomach churn the contents. The churning mixes the contents and makes them more fluid. Muscles at the end of the stomach allow food through slowly to the small intestine.

The small intestine is where most digestion takes place. It is divided into two main parts. The first is called the duodenum. Digestive juice from the pancreas flows into the duodenum. The juice has enzymes that digest proteins, carbohydrates and fats. Bile from the liver also flows into the duodenum. Bile helps with the digestion of fats.

The second part of the small intestine is the ileum. The ileum lining produces more enzymes to finish digestion. Most absorption of food takes place in the ileum. The lining has many fingerlike villi. The villi increase the surface area of the lining, which allows more absorption to take place.

The colon, or large intestine, absorbs water to form feces, but does not digest food. Feces leave the intestine through the anus. The appendix has little or no function in humans.

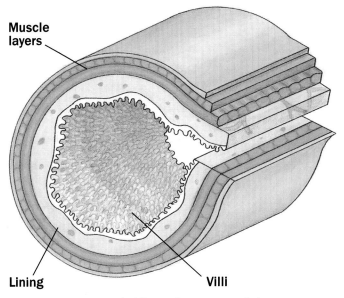

Muscle layers

Lining

Villi

△ Like other parts of the intestine, the ileum has muscles that move food along.

DID YOU KNOW?

Food spends a different length of time in each part of the intestine. The times vary, depending on the amount and type of food. For example, carbohydrate food spends less time in the stomach than protein food.

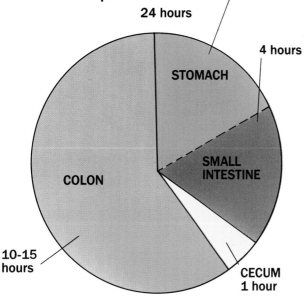

24 hours

1-4 hours

4 hours

STOMACH

SMALL INTESTINE

COLON

10-15 hours

CECUM 1 hour

WASTE PRODUCTS

Some of the food that is taken in cannot be used or stored by the body. Also, when food substances have been used, the remaining chemicals may be harmful. Some substances taken in, such as alcohol, may be poisonous. The removal of waste products and dangerous substances is known as excretion.

Proteins are not stored. If there is more protein than necessary in a meal, the extra is converted to carbohydrate. This conversion creates a by-product called urea that must be excreted.

The body converts other materials that it does not need into substances that can be excreted, including substances similar to urea and chemical salts. Most of the conversions take place in the liver.

The main organs of excretion are the two kidneys. They act as a kind of filter for the blood. The kidneys extract urea and similar substances, water and salts. These substances leave the body with water as urine.

STORAGE

Animals often absorb more food during digestion than they need right away. Animals store extra carbohydrates and fats, and some vitamins and minerals.

Digestion converts all carbohydrates to glucose (or similar sugars). If the body does not use glucose immediately, the liver and muscles convert it to a substance called glycogen. The body can change glycogen quickly back to glucose when it is needed. Only a small amount of glycogen is stored. Any more extra glucose is converted to fat.

Fats are stored as globules of fat in special fat cells. There are fat cells in most organs of the body and especially under the skin. The body can store very large amounts of fat. The fat acts as a long-term energy store.

△ Stored fat seen with a powerful miscroscope.

PROJECT

When you cut an apple, the cut surface turns brown after a while. This is the result of an enzyme-controlled reaction. The reaction takes place with air. Enzymes are very sensitive to acidity. If the acidity is wrong, they will not work. Ask an adult for a knife and cut an apple in half. Rub the cut surface of one half with lemon juice (which is acidic). Leave the apple for half an hour. The half with lemon juice will not have turned brown. Now eat the apple!

△ Penguins give their young partly-digested food.

▷ Birds have crops and gizzards; mammals do not.

Gizzard — Intestine — Liver — Crop

VARIATIONS

Animal digestive systems vary. Amoebas (page 12) have no real digestive system. Simple animals, such as jellyfish, have a gut but with no different parts. More complex animals, such as insects, have digestive systems with several sections. Animals such as fish, reptiles and birds have systems with many or most of the parts that humans have. They may also have parts that humans do not have.

Birds, for example, have a crop in which food is stored. Birds also have a gizzard, which is a muscular bag. It contains small stones that the bird has swallowed. The gizzard churns food and the stones together to break up the food. The digestive system of some young birds is poorly developed. The adult birds feed the young with partly digested food.

Mammals — such as dogs, cats, rabbits and sheep — have digestive systems with all the parts of a human system. Sometimes parts are larger or smaller. For example, a rabbit has a much larger cecum and appendix (page 14). Another example, is the extra "stomachs" of ruminants (page 15), which are really pouches in the esophagus.

DID YOU KNOW?

The caterpillar of a cinnabar moth feeds on ragwort. Instead of excreting poison from the ragwort, it keeps the poison in its body to put off predators.

Animals need energy for everything they do. They need it for such things as movement, but also for all the chemical reactions in the body. Animals get energy from food. The amount of food they need depends on the kind of body they have and on their behavior. Some animals also need to store large amounts of food.

ENERGY NEEDS

An animal that is very active uses up more energy than one that is not moving. For example, a bird uses much more energy while flying than if it is sitting on its nest. An animal that uses a lot of energy during a day needs to eat more food than one that uses little energy. For example, a human sitting down all day might need to eat food containing 10,000 joules of energy; somebody doing physical work all day might need 15,000 joules. You may have noticed that you are more hungry if you have been playing sports than if you have been watching television all day.

Mammals and birds use energy to keep their bodies warm. Other animals rely mostly on heat from their surroundings. Small mammals and birds need more energy to keep warm than large animals need. This is because a small animal has a larger surface area in relation to its volume. A large surface area means that an animal loses heat quickly. As a result,

△ Shrews need to eat very large amounts of food.

a shrew may eat more than three times its own body weight in food every day; an elephant eats only a small part of its own weight in food each day.

Some animals eat large meals for other reasons. Eating a very large meal means that an animal does not have to use energy to find more food for a long time. The disadvantage is that it may be so full that it can hardly move! Some blood-sucking animals eat very large meals. For example, leeches can suck more than their body weight of blood in one meal. This is largely because leeches only rarely find hosts.

◁ Some large snakes can swallow a whole antelope. Part of the reason is that snakes do not have teeth that can break up prey. But an enormous meal gives a snake a huge supply of energy that will last it for a long period of time.

ENERGY SUPPLIES

Animals need to store food for times when food is not available. Food for energy is stored mostly as fat inside an animal's body.

Animals need to store small amounts of fat to give themselves energy between meals. This is necessary even when there is plenty of food available because, for example, a lion might fail in its hunting for a few days. Fat may be stored for much longer. A good example of a long-term fat store is a camel's hump. Camels may not eat for many days in desert land.

Winter is a time when there is a shortage of food for many animals. It is common to build up supplies of fat during the summer. These supplies keep animals alive during the winter months.

Some animals, such as bears and dormice, hibernate which means that they sleep all through winter. When animals hibernate, the processes in their bodies (such as the heartbeat) become very slow. This not only means that they use up very little energy, but also that they do not need to look for or eat food. Animals that hibernate must build up large supplies of fat.

A few animals store food outside their bodies. For example, squirrels hide nuts and similar food. In the same way, bees store food in the form of honey.

△ Dormice and many other animals hibernate in winter.

△ A camel's hump is a large store of food energy.

PROJECT

You may eat a wider variety of food than you realize. Make notes of all the food you eat. Write down the ingredients of any mixed foods. You can get help with this by reading the labels on food packets or asking the person who made the food. At the end of a week, see how often you ate each kind of food. Find out if what you eat in a second week is very different or about the same as in the first.

Animals have a myriad of techniques of feeding and they eat a great variety of food. In any environment, it is usually possible to find animals that eat every kind of food available.

Honey possums are an example of an unusual animal that takes advantage of a good food source. Honey possums are the only mammals that feed on nothing but the nectar and pollen in flowers. They live in parts of southwest Australia where there are plants flowering all year around. This means that they have a constant supply of food.

Some animals eat food that is not normally found in their environment. An example is archer fish, which live in tropical areas. Many fish eat insects that

△ Honey possums have a long, brush-tipped tongue.

live in water. Archer fish eat insects that live on land. An archer fish shoots jets of water from its mouth at insects on leaves and branches over the water. The jet knocks the insects into the water, and the fish eats them.

There are even some animals that are cannibals. The praying mantis is an example. After a female mantis has mated with a male, she usually eats her mate. Another example is that when a shark is killed, other sharks of the same type may eat its body. Most animals never eat other animals of the same type.

The strangest feeders of all are perhaps humans. No other animal cooks its food and uses recipes. Humans have farms and many more methods of hunting, storing and transporting food than any other animal.

△ Archer fish shoot jets of water at insects.

◁ The female praying mantis has mouthparts for cutting and chewing. She uses these with deadly effect on male mantises after mating.

When waiting for an unwary insect, the mantis — whose name comes from the Greek word "prophet" — stands motionless as if in prayer. But because of the way this voracious creature captures and devours its victims, a better name might have been "preying" mantis!

carnivore
An animal that eats only other animals.

cell
The basic unit that makes up all living tissue. There are many different types of cell, for example, liver cells.

diet
The food that an animal eats.

digestion
The chemical breakdown of food. Digestion breaks down food into substances that can be absorbed and used by an animal's body.

energy
The ability to do work. The work might be lifting a heavy object, or it might be a chemical reaction that changes one substance into another.

enzyme
A biological catalyst. A catalyst is a substance that makes a chemical reaction happen more quickly, but without being changed itself. Many enzymes are involved in digestion.

food
Anything that an animal eats and that contains nutrients.

herbivore
An animal that eats only plants.

host
A living plant or animal that a parasite feeds off.

intestine
A tube-like passage in an animal's body in which food is digested and absorbed. In most animals, the intestine has a number of different parts. It is also known as the gut.

mammal
An animal that has a backbone, warm blood, gives birth to live young, and feeds its young on milk. Humans, dogs, sheep and whales are all mammals.

nutrient
A substance in an animal's food that is absorbed and used by the animal's body. For example, vitamins and fats are both nutrients.

omnivore
An animal that eats both plants and other animals.

organ
A part of the body of an animal that has one or more particular functions. For example, the liver is an organ. Most organs are made up of a number of special kinds of tissue.

organism
Any living thing, for example, a plant, an amoeba, a bird or an elephant. Most organisms are made up of a number of organs.

parasite
An animal that feeds off another plant or animal while that plant or animal is still alive.

predator
An animal that hunts other animals for its food.

prey
An animal that a predator hunts and kills for its food.

tissue
A group of cells of the same type, all of which have a particular function or group of functions. For example, liver tissue or skin tissue.

Photographic Credits:
All the pictures in this book have been supplied by Bruce Coleman Limited apart from: page 14: Flick Killerby; pages 19, 20-21, 23 top and bottom and 30 bottom: Planet Earth Pictures; page 26: Science Photo Library.

PRINTED IN BELGIUM BY

INTERNATIONAL BOOK PRODUCTION